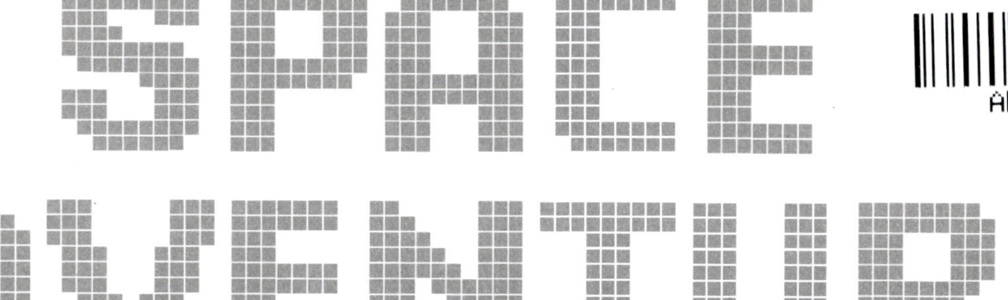

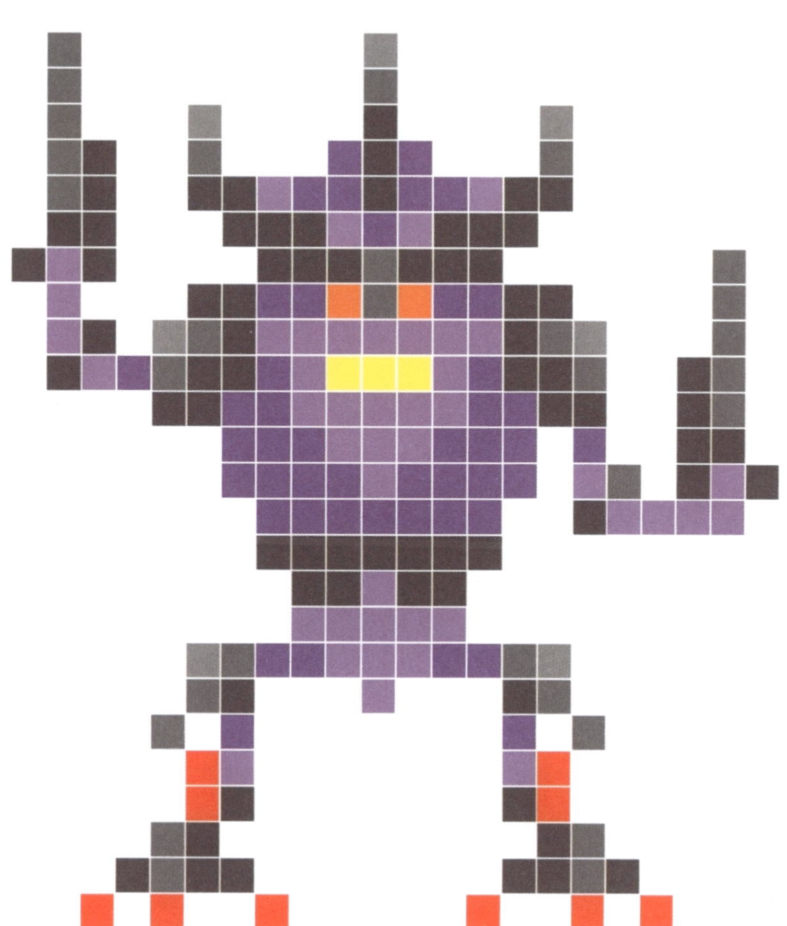

Illustrated by Barry Green
Written by Joshua George

Licensed exclusively to Top That Publishing Ltd
Tide Mill Way, Woodbridge, Suffolk, IP12 1AP, UK
www.topthatpublishing.com

2 4 6 8 9 7 5 3 1
Manufactured in China

Spaceship 'Quantum'

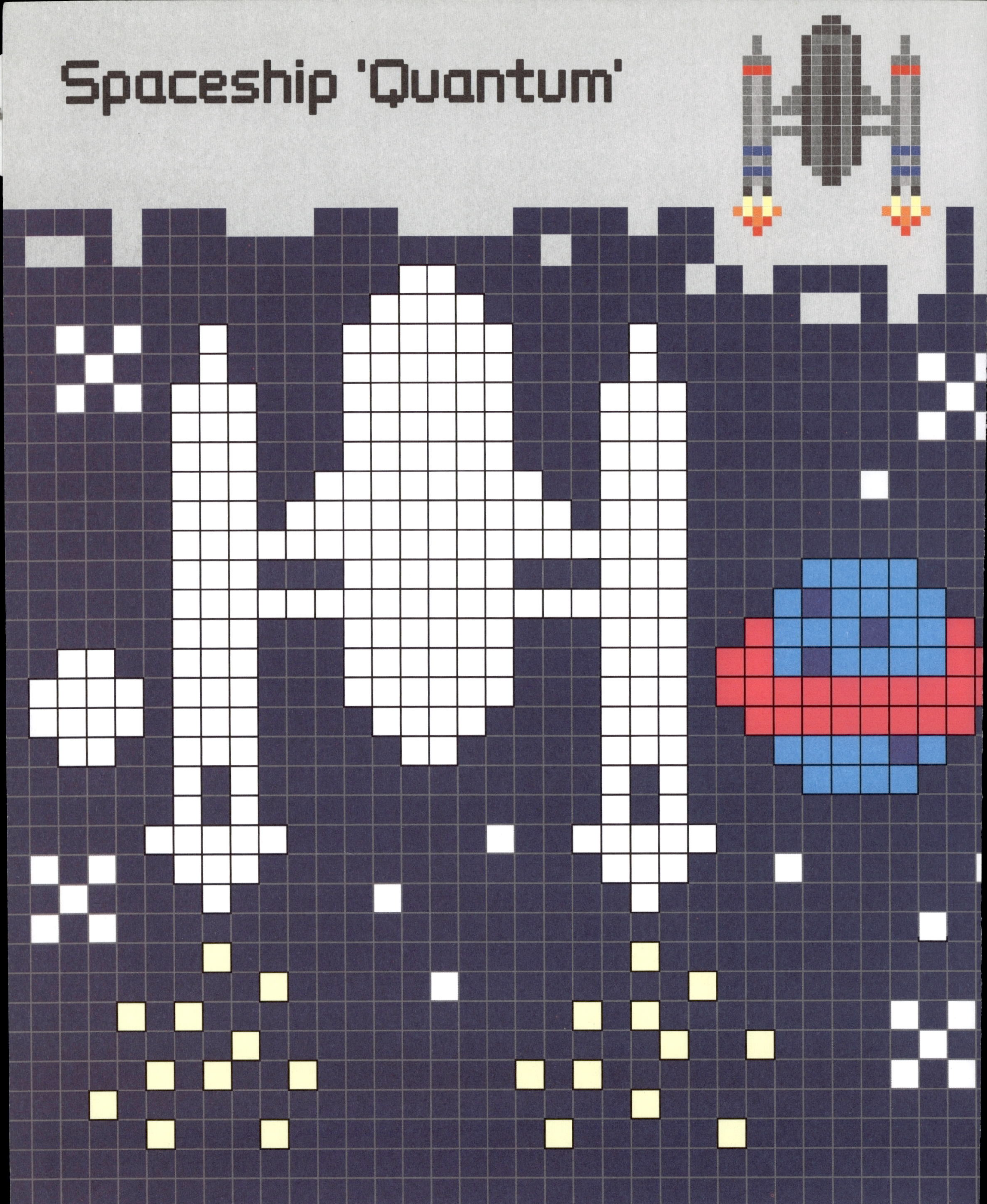

This spaceship is the pride of the Galactic Empire. Its mighty engines blast it through space at light speed! Whoosh!

Speeder

If you need to get from one planet to another fast, I'll take you in my speeder, but it will cost you! Hold on tight!

These awesome mining machines travel the outer galaxy in search of precious metals and minerals. Start the drills!

Battleship

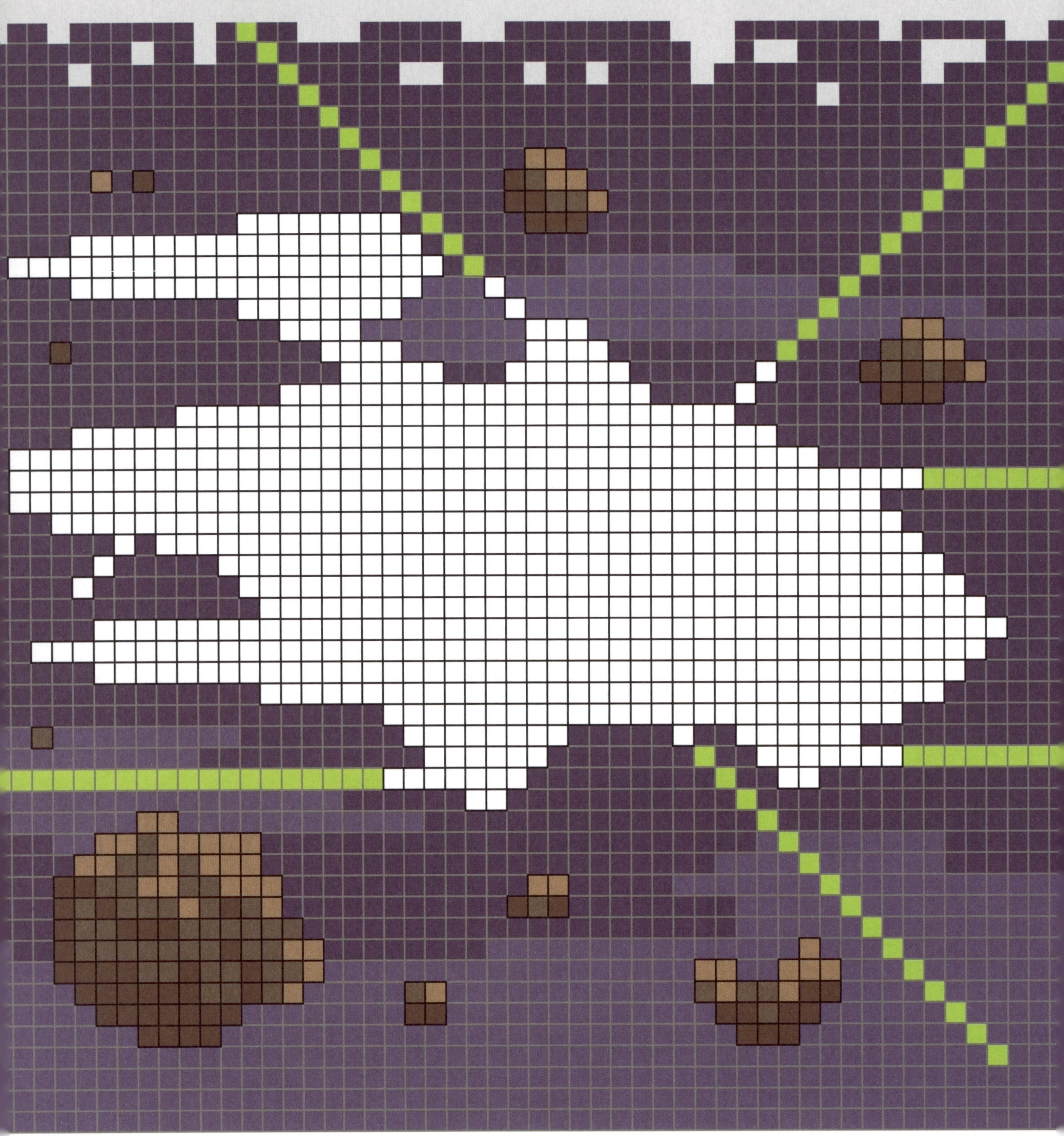

This battleship is state-of-the-art. It's testing out its new pulsar cannons on some passing asteroids. Watch out! Ka-blam!

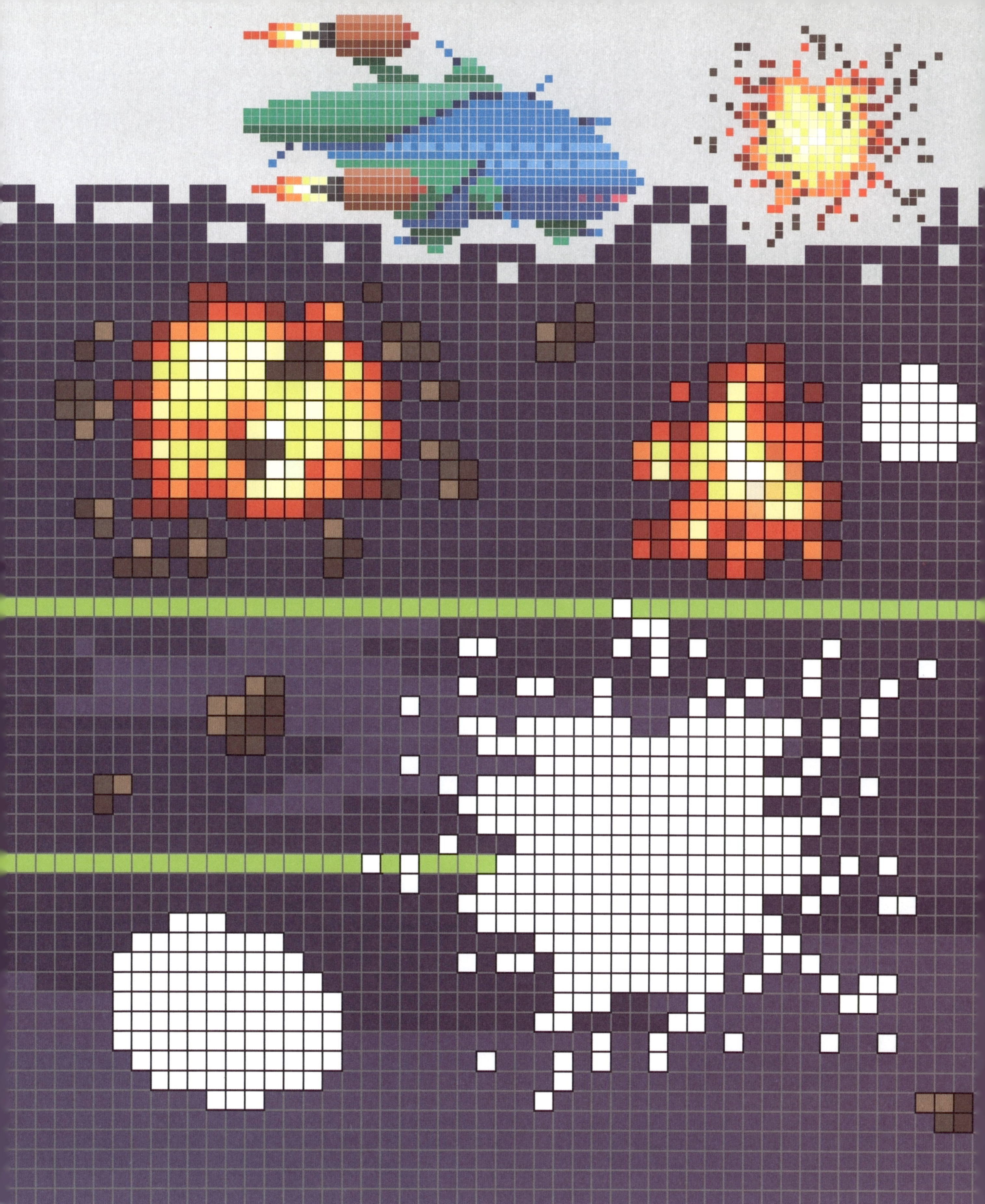

Mega Brain

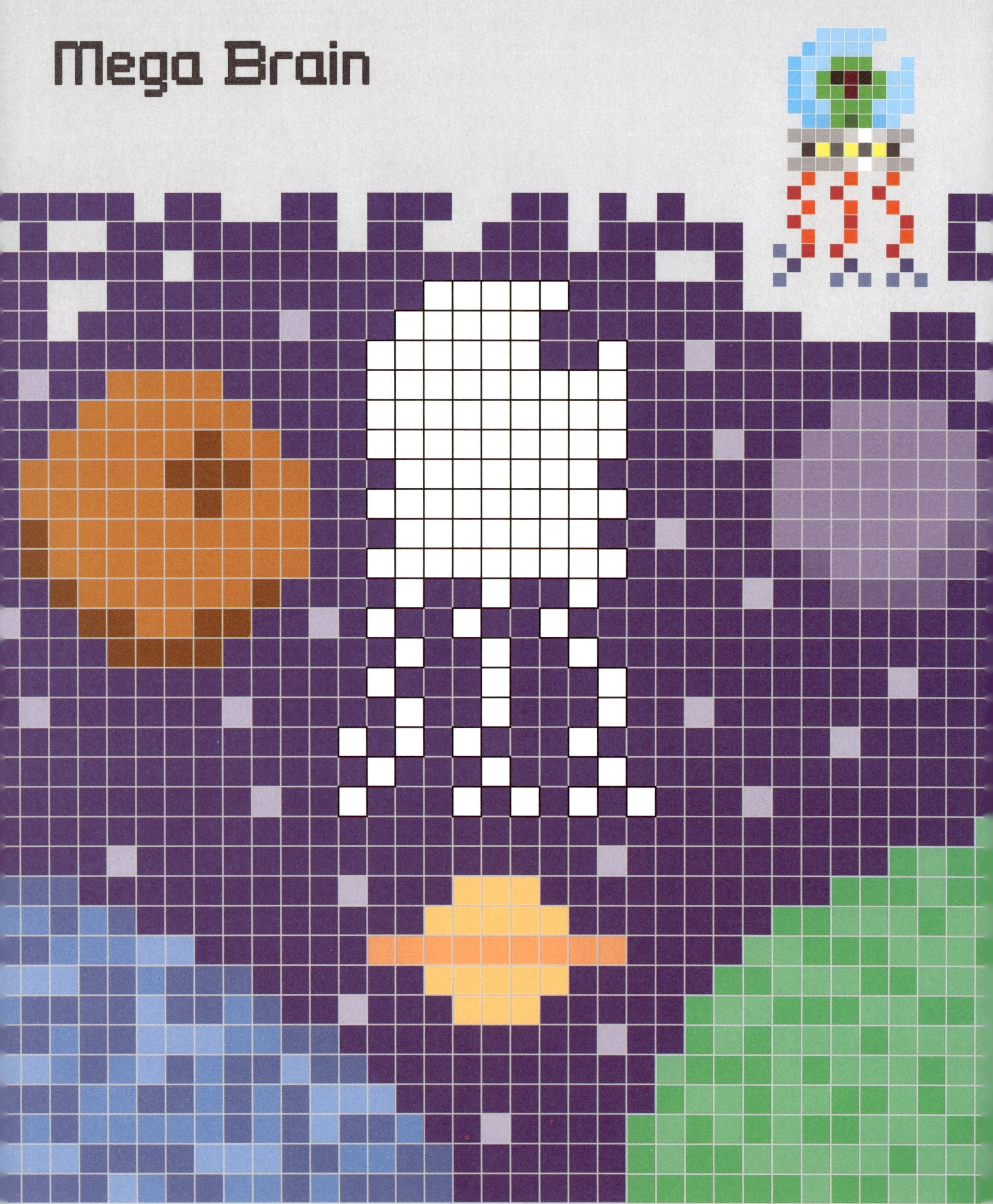

An extraterrestrial brain fitted to a robotic body, Mega Brain comes from the Plexsus Nebula in search of a new home. Bzzzzzzz!

Captain Chaos

I'm a deep space flying ace in my supersonic fighter. I keep the galaxy safe from invaders by blasting them to smithereens. Take that!

Solar Sailor

Ahoy there! My craft is powered by solar rays. It's slow to accelerate but can reach enormous speeds.

Space Pirate

Space pirates roam the galaxy looking for unarmed ships to attack. Warp the plank!

Neutreno

Neutreno is the super-intelligent leader of an alien alliance from the edge of the Basmat system ... prepare to meet your maker, earthling!

Rocket

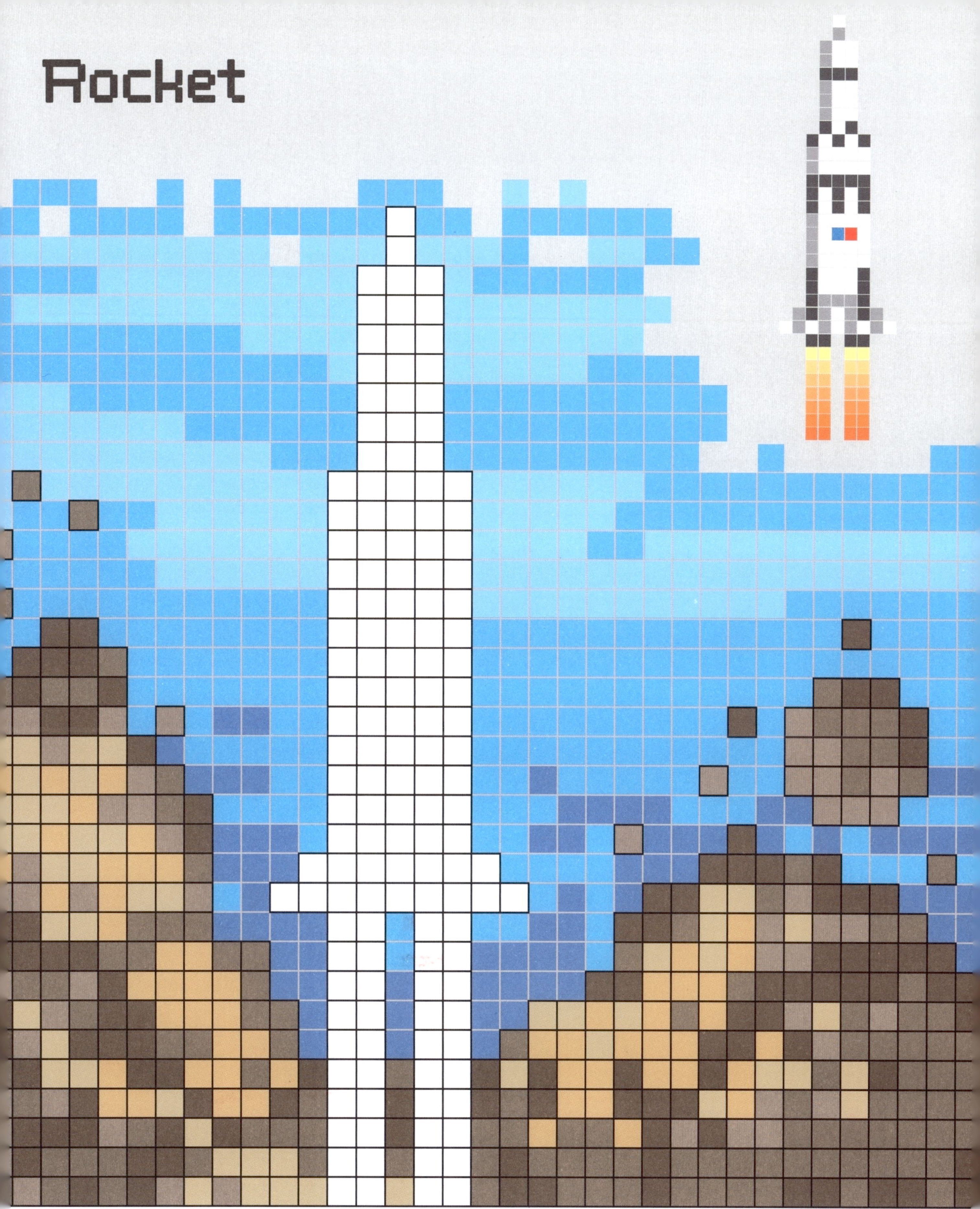

3 ... 2 ... 1 ... Lift off! In the distant future, some people like to fly rockets from the ancient past. This 21st century rocket is so old-fashioned!

Battle Droids

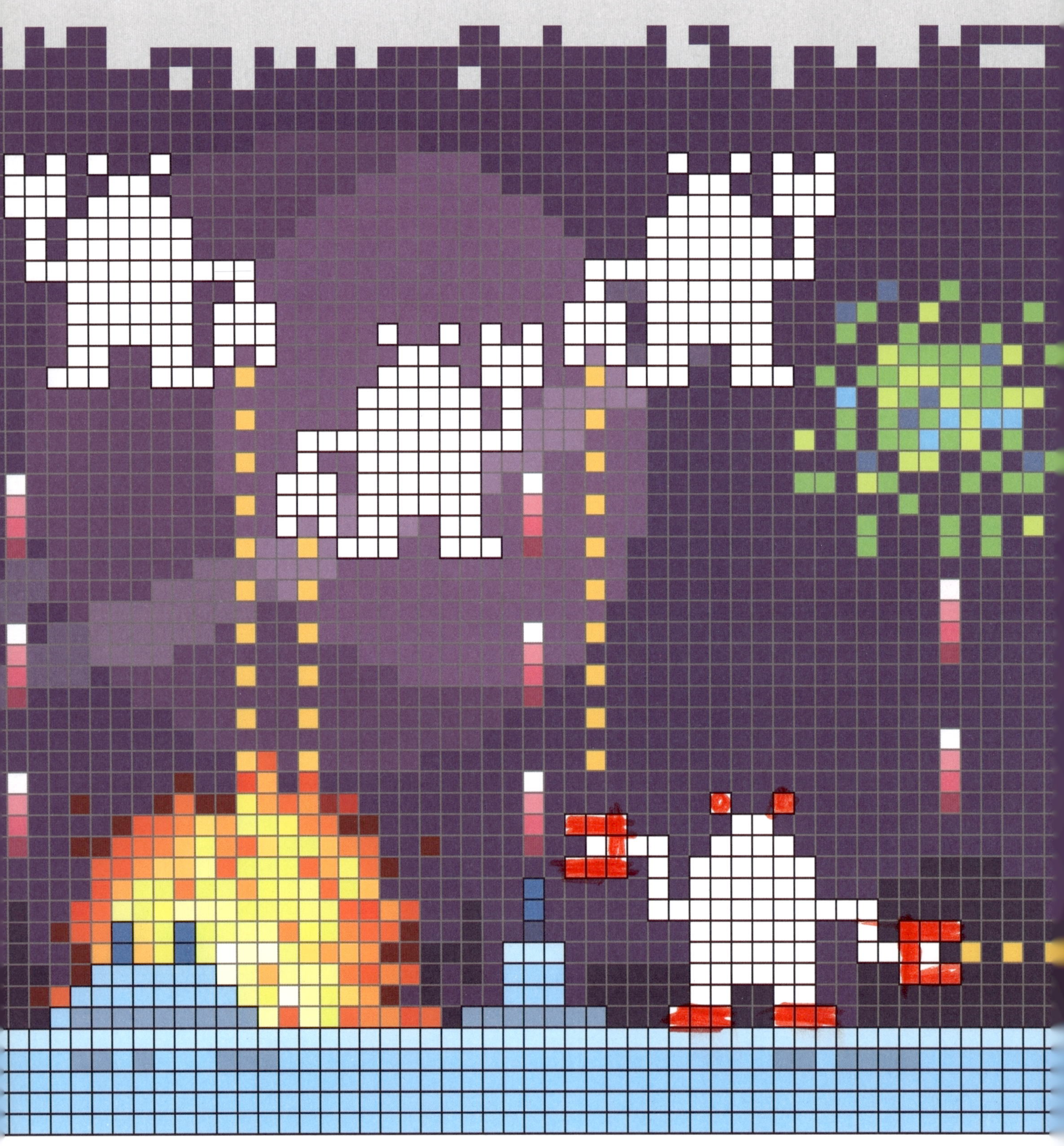

Destroy! Destroy! Battle Droids roam the galaxy destroying any threat to the Galactic Empire.

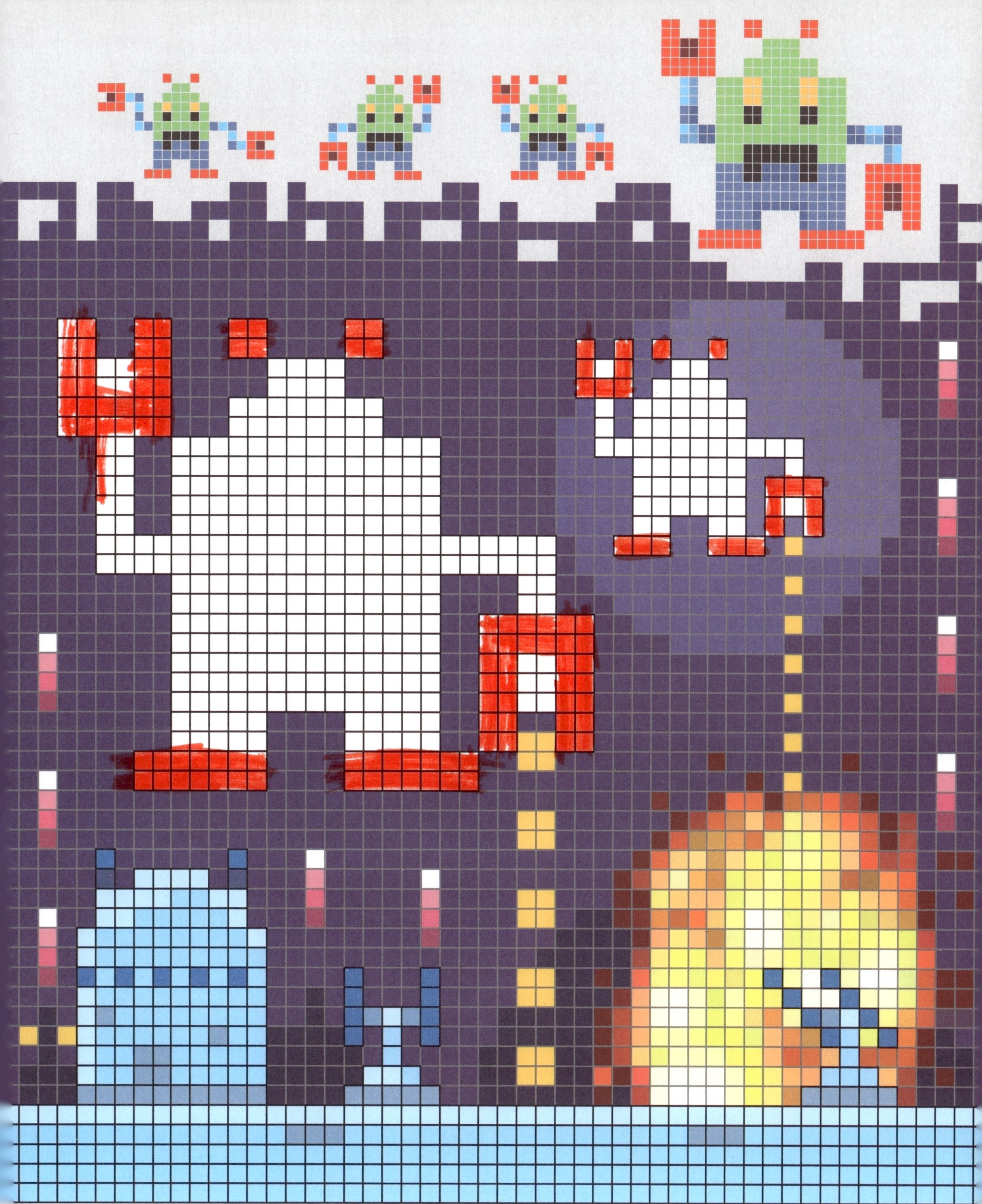

Arachnid

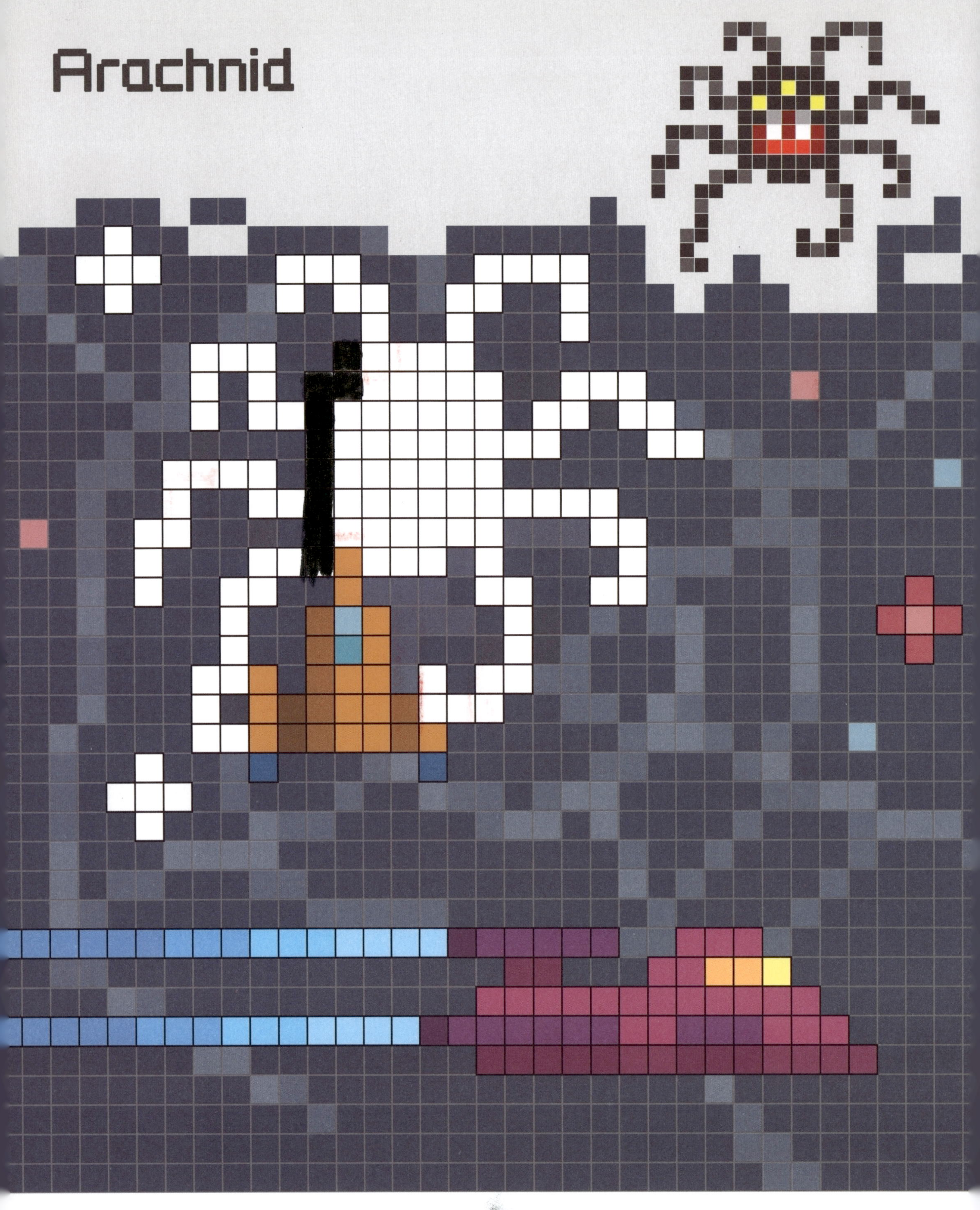

Dinner Time! Arachnid is a massive eight-legged alien that lives in outer space. He catches his prey in enormous space webs.

Bounty Hunter

Surrender, scum! Bounty Hunter will work for anyone that pays! His laser gun and rocket boots make him a deadly enemy.

The Blip

Blip ... blip ... BOOM! I'm just a blip on your screen – an unidentified flying object. I whizz through space, looking for new civilisations ... to destroy!

Starsuit

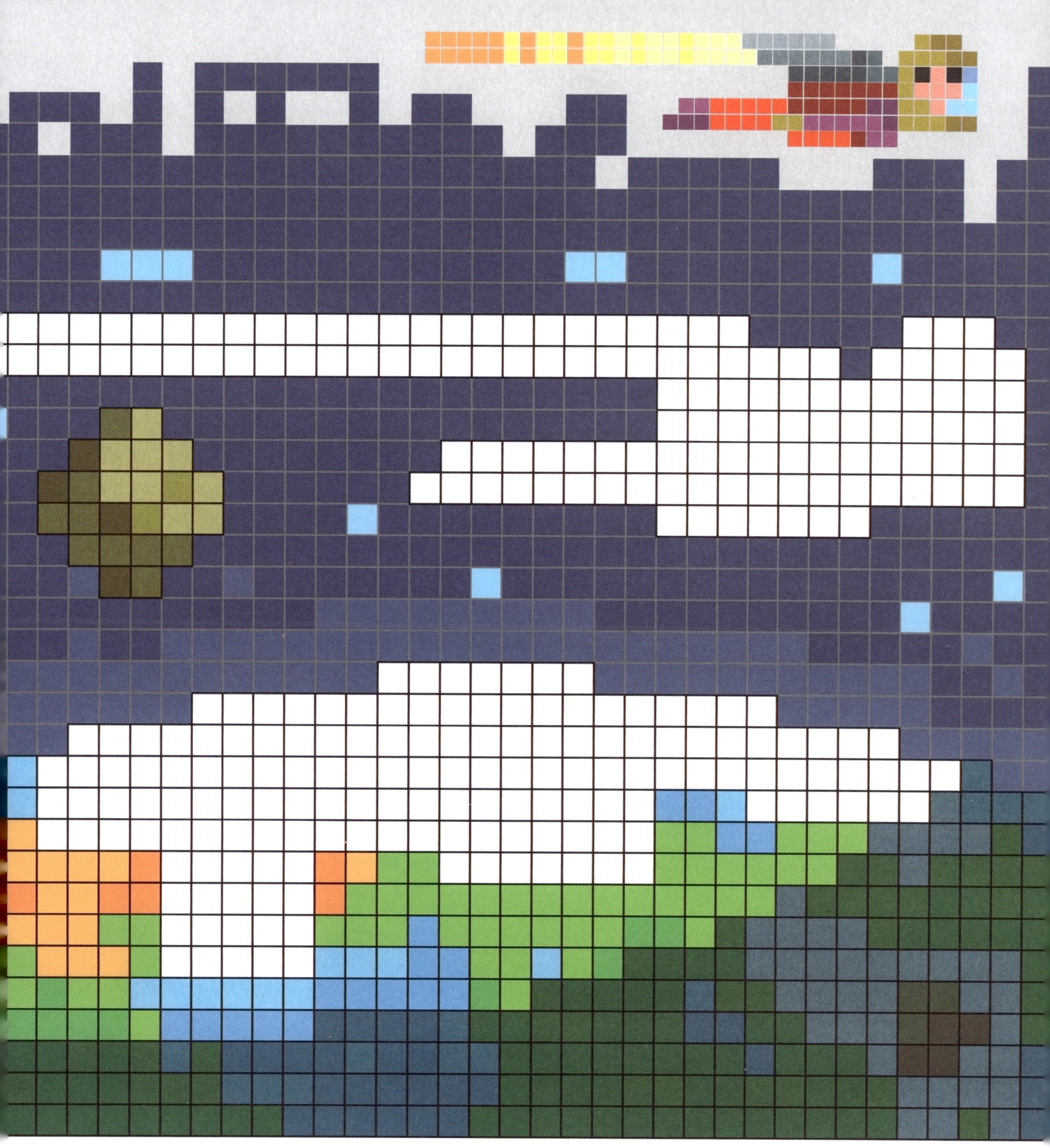

Maximum Speed! A starsuit is a special spacesuit that can fly short distances through space. It looks like this guy is in a hurry!

Rampaging Robot

Beep, beep, beep! This huge robot has gone on the rampage! It's destroying everything in its way with its red laser-beam eyes!

Apocalypse

Apocalypse's asteroid home was destroyed by a rogue mining craft. Now he's sworn to destroy the galaxy! Mwa ha ha!

Interceptor

I'm called out when an unidentified ship is spotted. My ship is fast and well-armed and I mean business! State your name and purpose!

Lord Blob

Lord Blob has declared war on the Star Council. Things could get nasty! Bow down to your new lord!

Incoming!

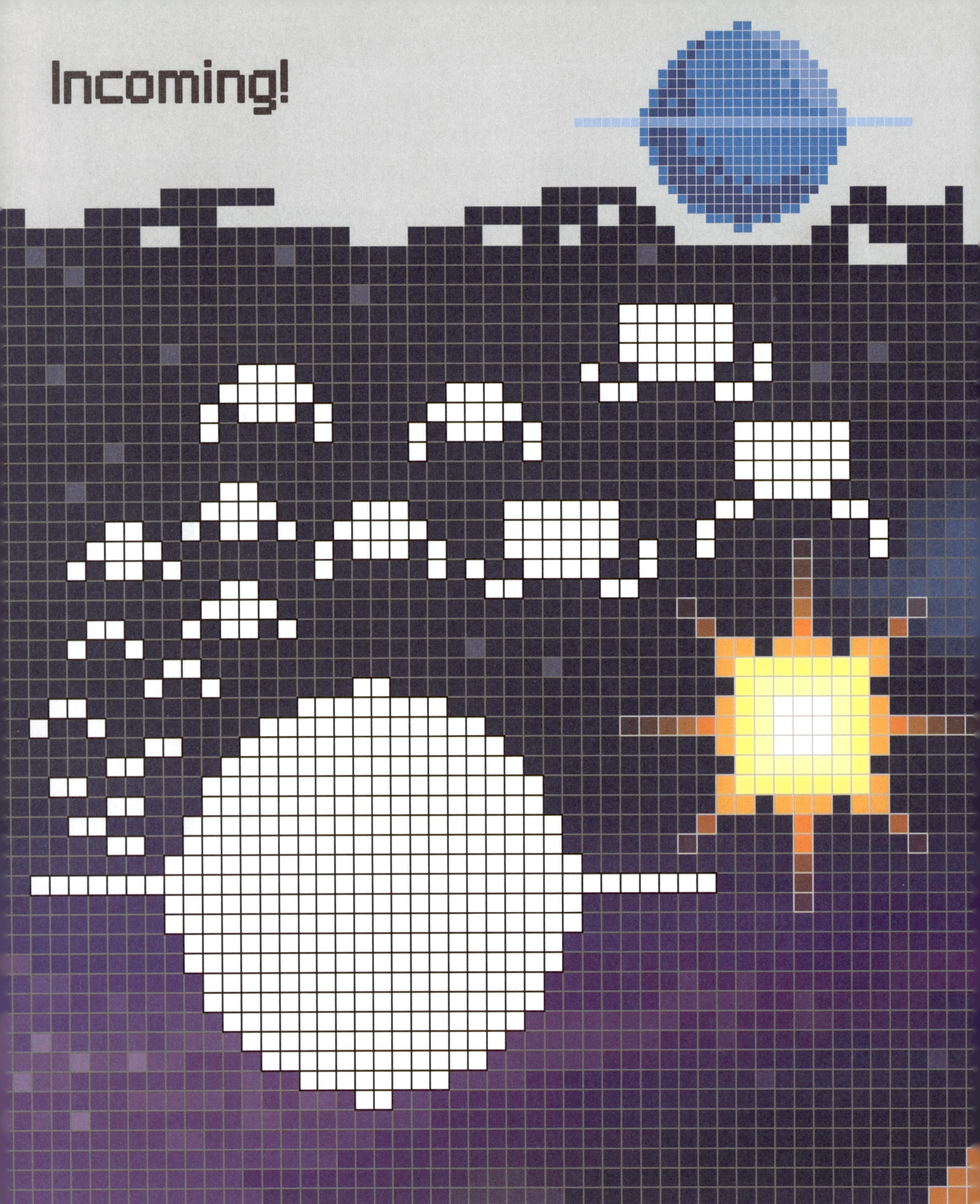

The Space Station is picking up a number of unidentified flying objects. They're not slowing down, Captain! Bleep, bleep, bleep!

Space Station Command

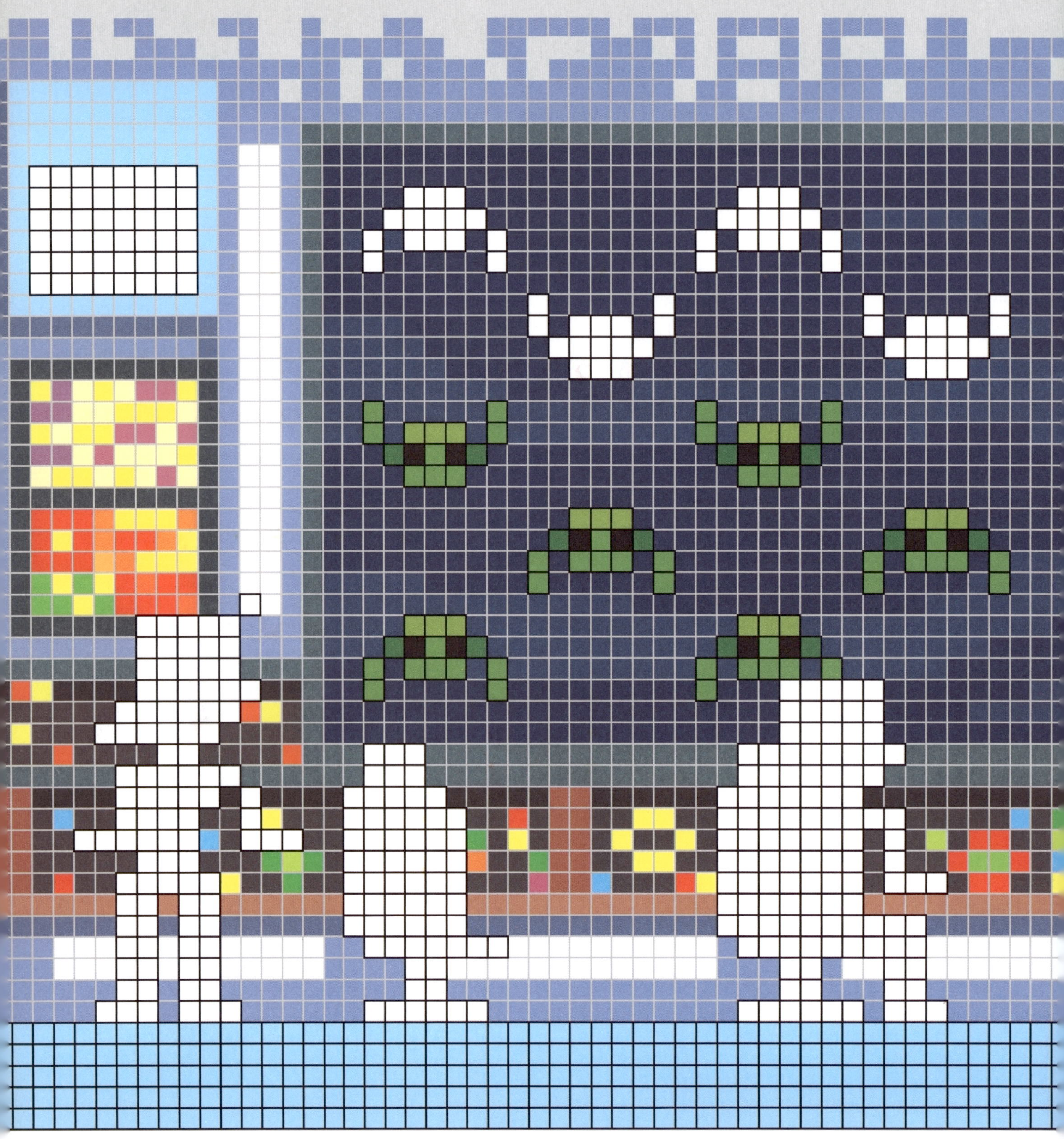

This is the captain speaking ... the Space Station is under attack! All crew report to positions! Repeat, all crew report to positions!

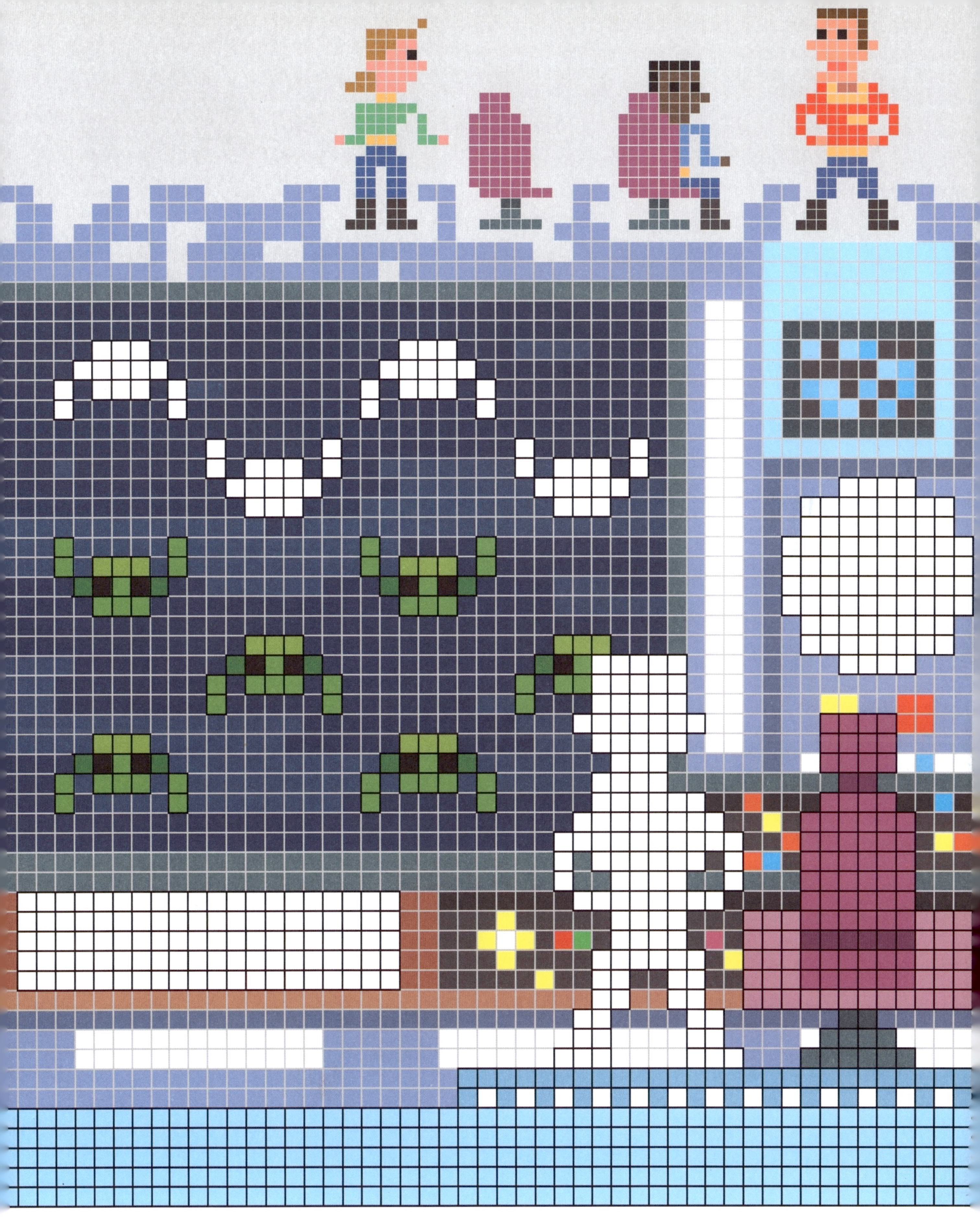

Scramble Fighters

The Space Station fighter craft have been scrambled to meet the attack, but they are heavily outnumbered.

Star Tanks

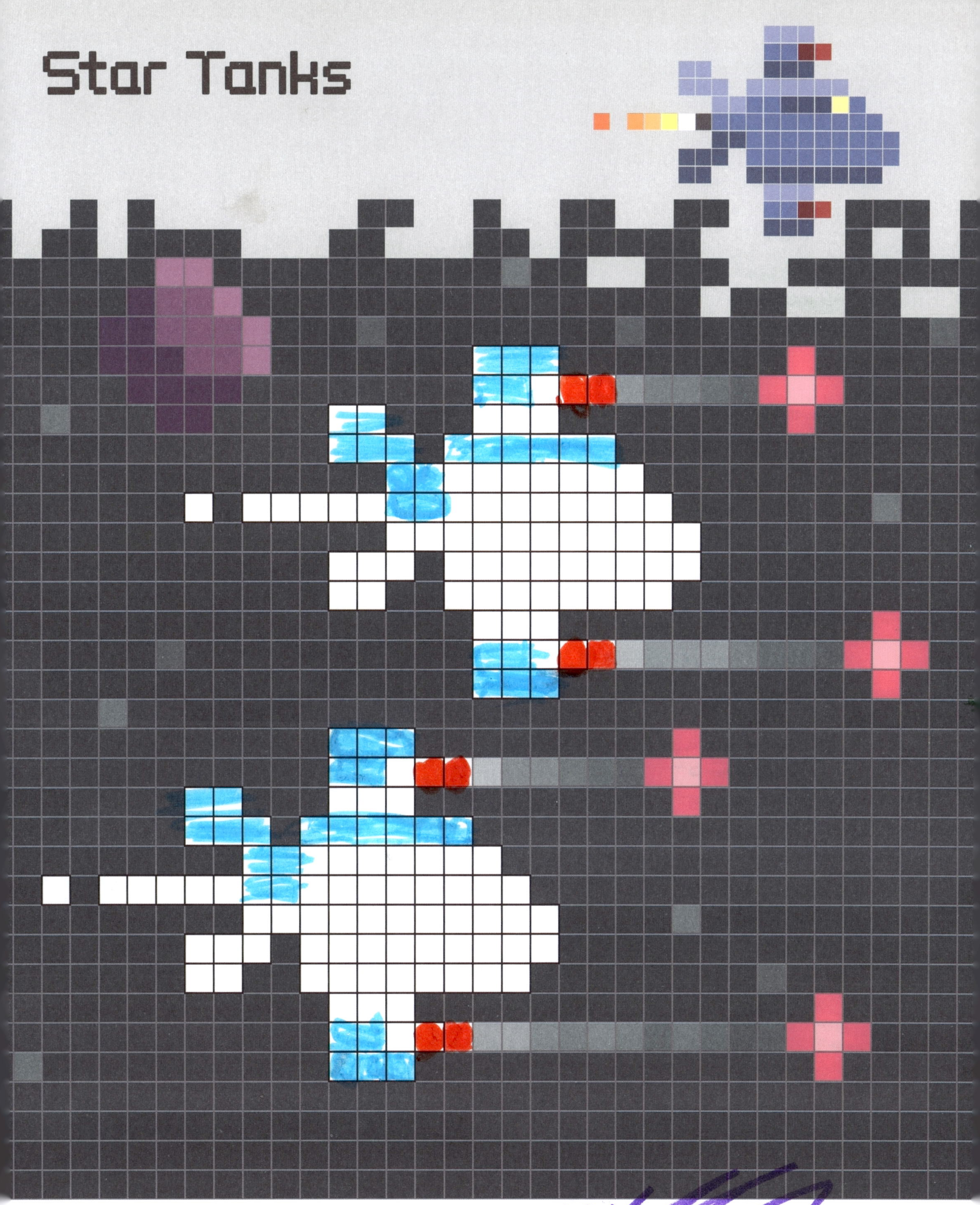

The Space Station only has a few star tanks and they are very slow, but their laser cannons pack a powerful punch. Blam! Blam! Blam!

Destroyer

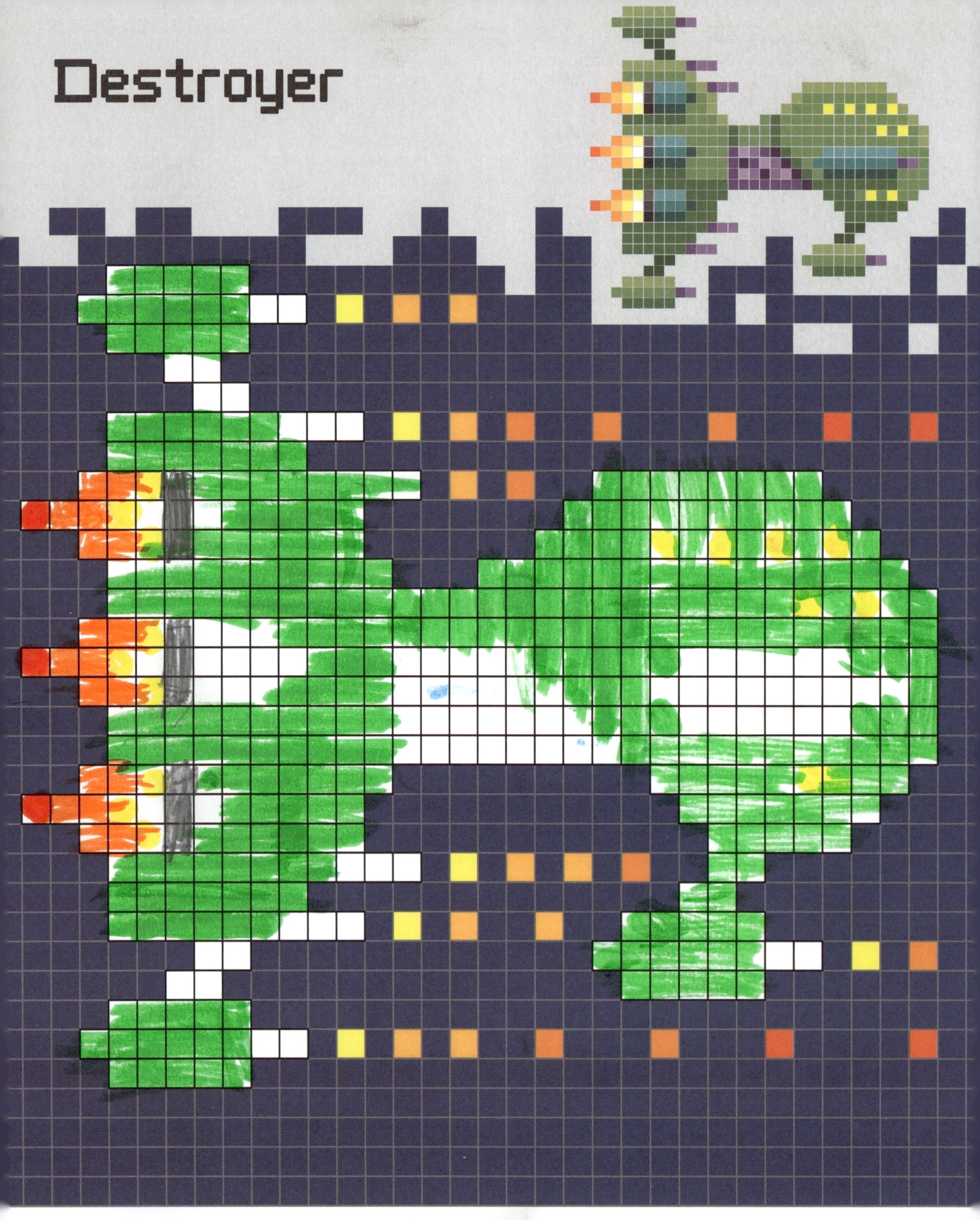

The Battle Fleet is on its way! This massive destroyer is leading the fleet into the battle. Surrender or be destroyed!

Troop Carrier

When the Battle Fleet needs to transport troopers, it uses these enormous carrier vessels. All troops report to the loading bay!

Space Battle

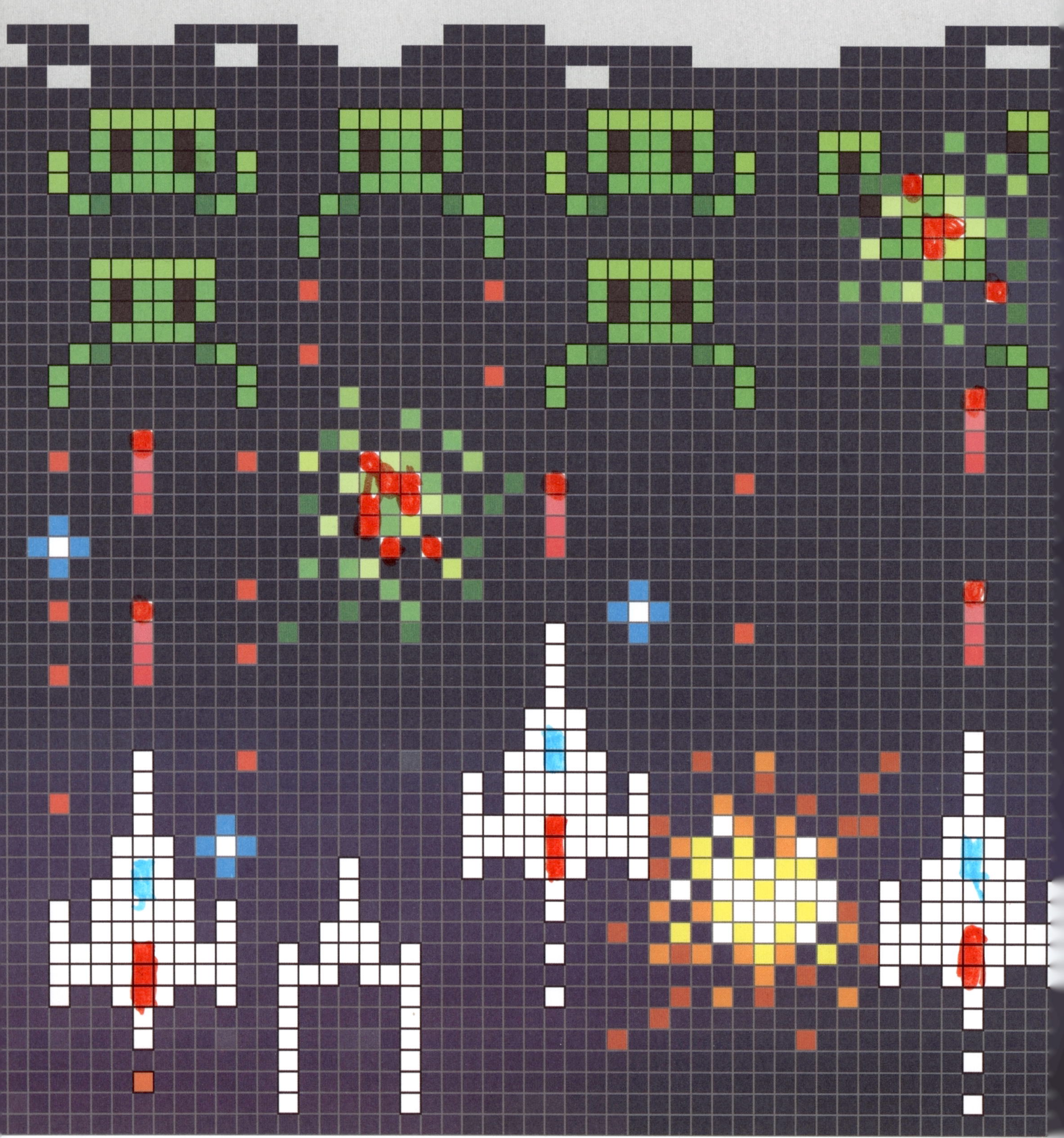

The Space Station fighters are desperately holding back the Blob attack. Pow! Pow! Zap! Zap! Pow!

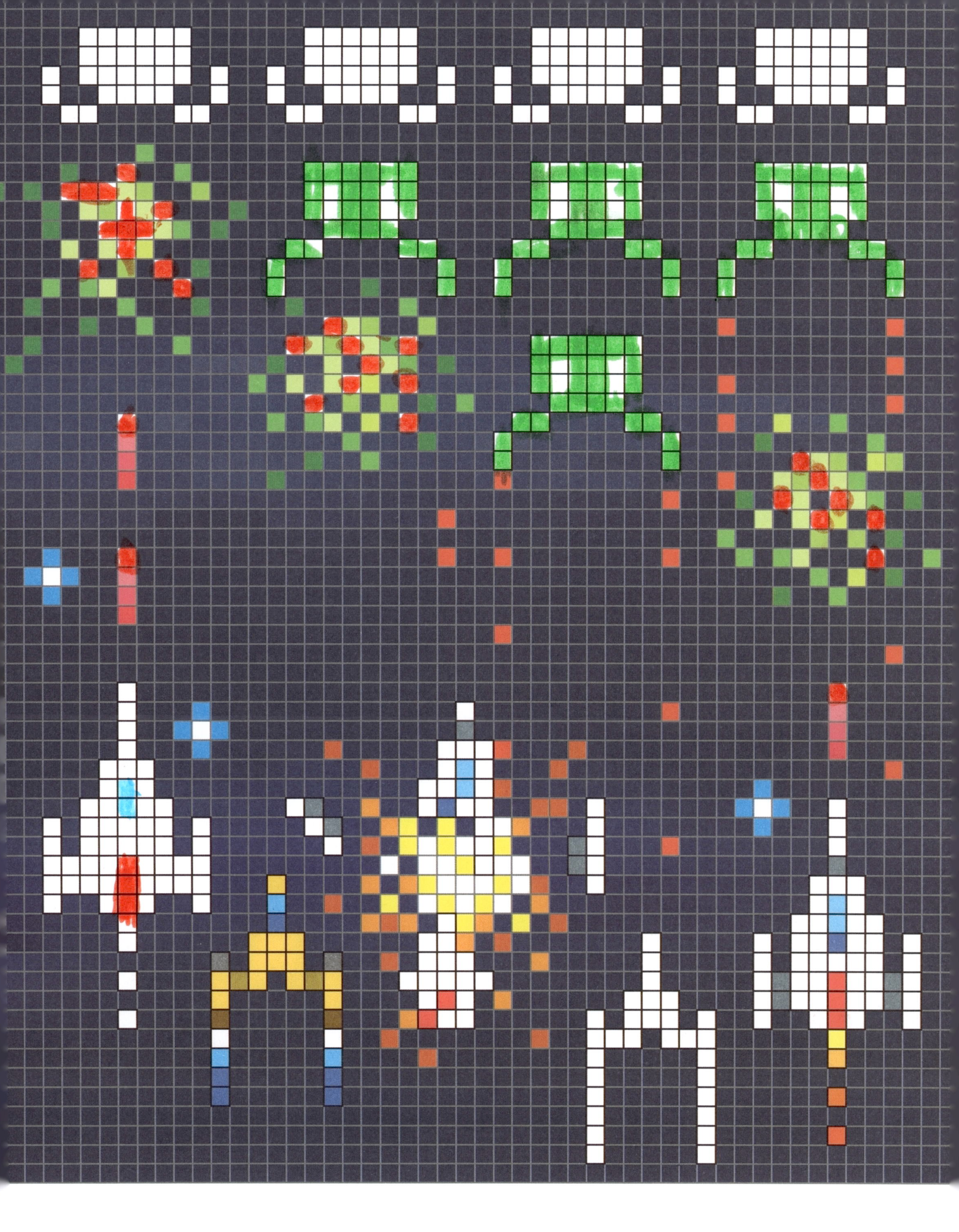

Victory

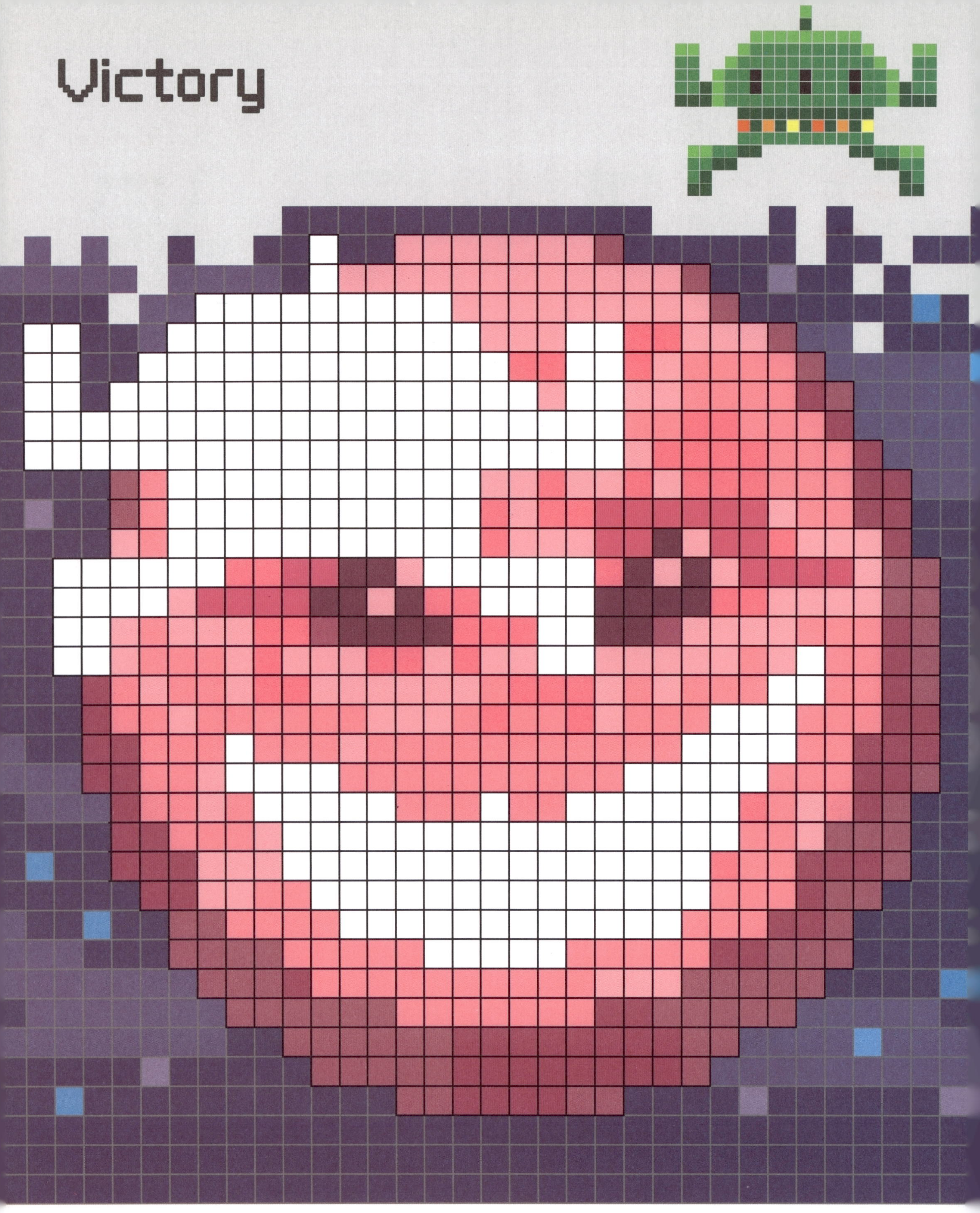

The Battle Fleet troops arrived and defeated Lord Blob's army. But nobody has spotted Lord Blob fleeing to safety. Next time, earthlings!

Mongo the Merciless

Mongo the Merciless has captured a lost fighter craft, and now he's started to eat it! Munch, munch!

Moondusa

On the dark side of a small moon lives someone you really don't want to meet! Moondusa and her terrifying space-snake hair! Sssss!

Escape Pod

Aiiiieeeeeeeee! When my ship malfunctioned I had to escape in this tiny escape pod. Now I'm re-entering the atmosphere of the planet Xantar.

Galumph

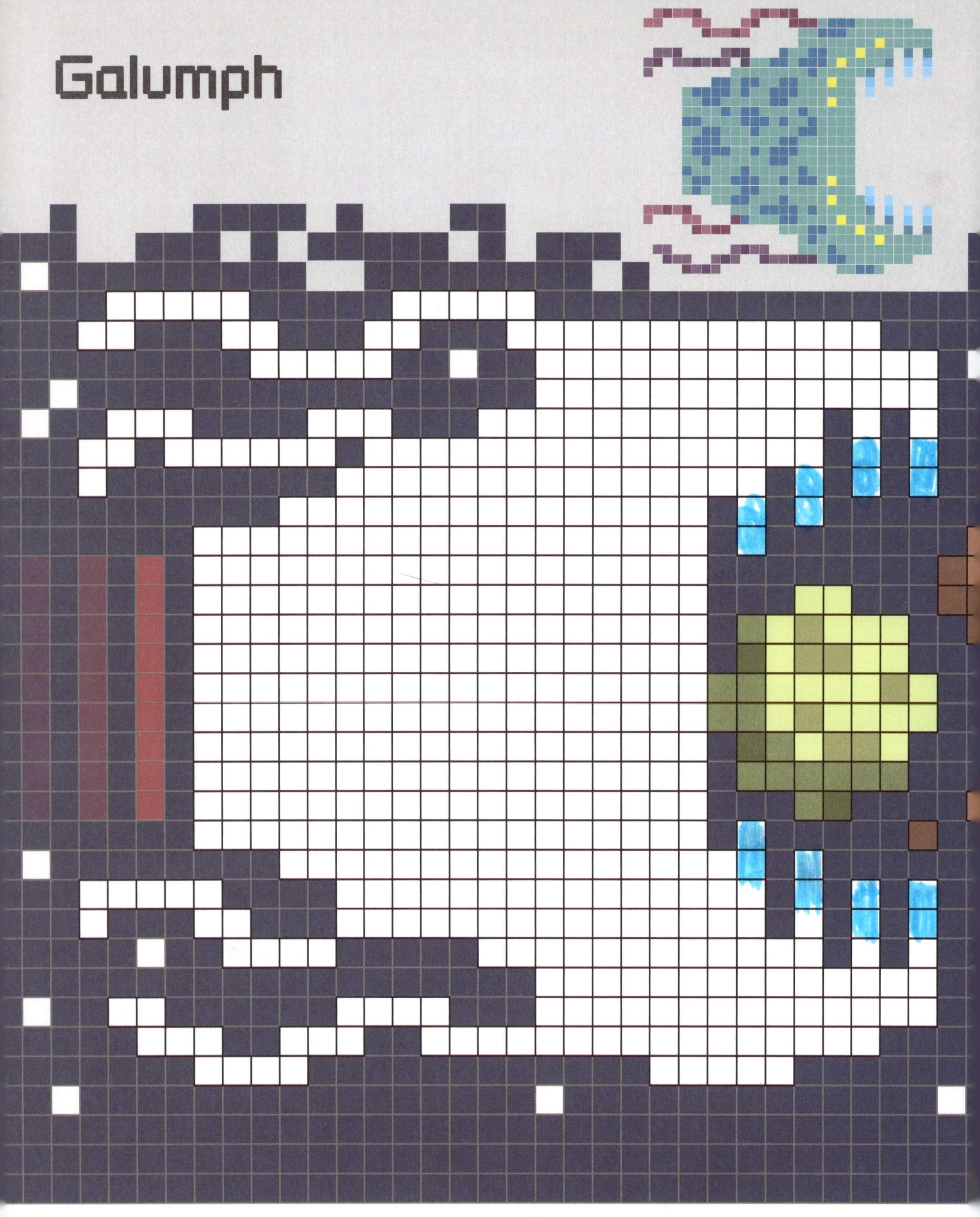

Galumph is the biggest life form ever discovered. He floats through space eating asteroids and small moons. Chomp, chomp!

Spaceship 'X'

Spaceship 'X' is the Battle Fleet's top-secret new craft. It's powered by thought and can travel instantly across the universe. Hold tight!

Meteor Shower

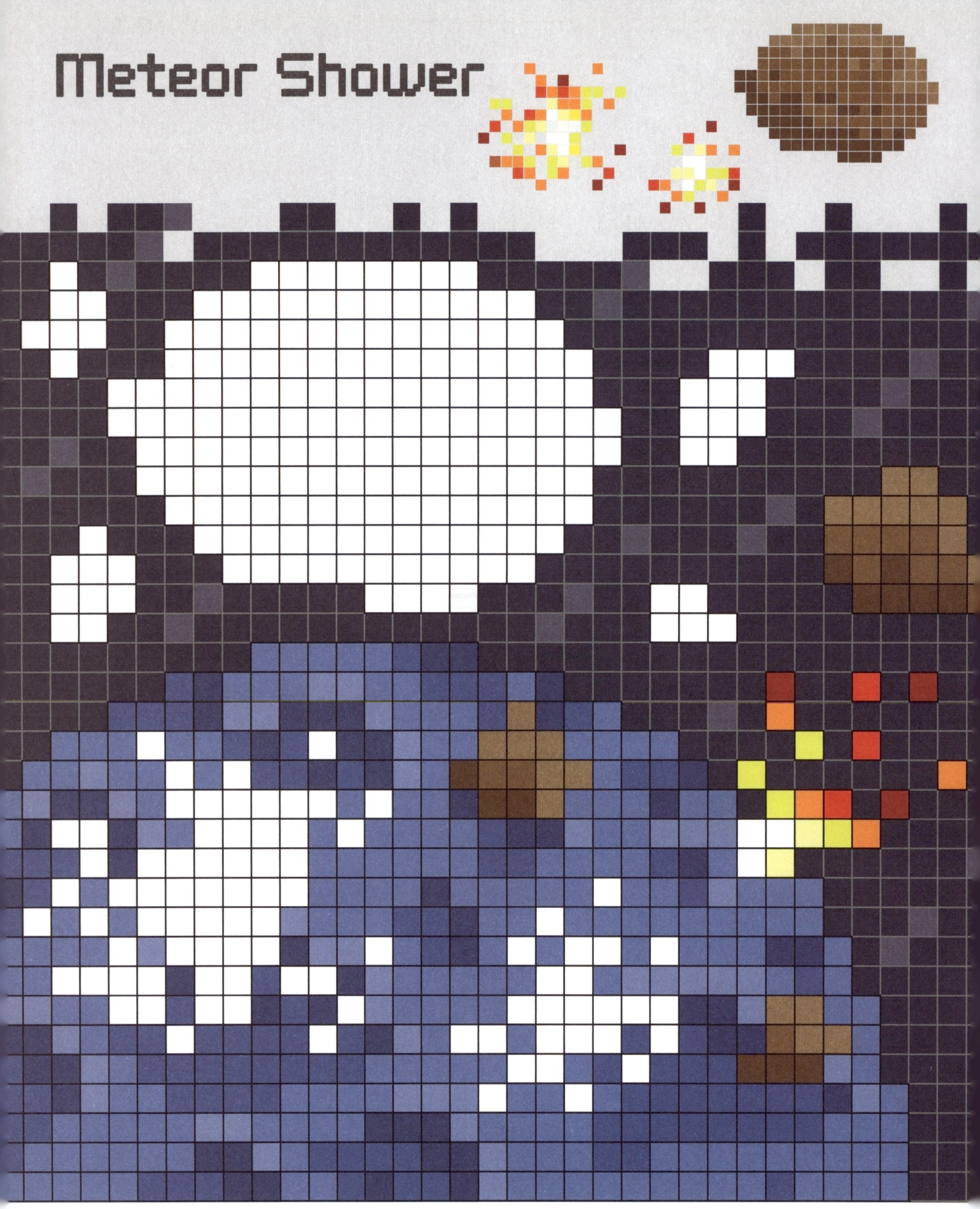

Hold on! This planet is being hit by flying space rocks! You can feel the impacts from here!

Spaceship Repair

This spaceship has hit some space junk and needs urgent repairs before it can continue. Clunk! Clunk!

Space Dragons

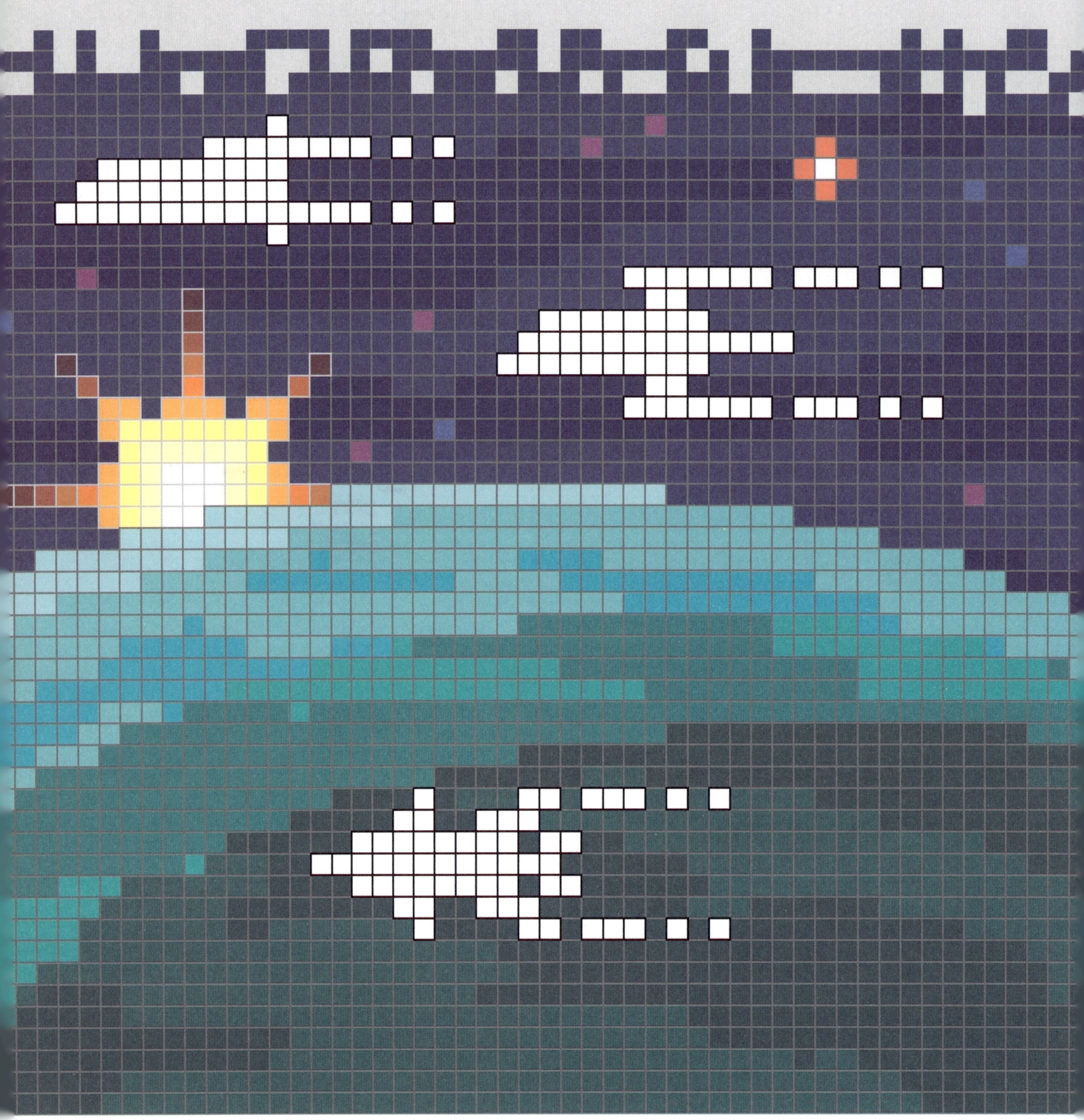

Uh-oh! Don't look now, but there seems to be some space dragons behind us. Hopefully they're not hungry!

Infantry Droid

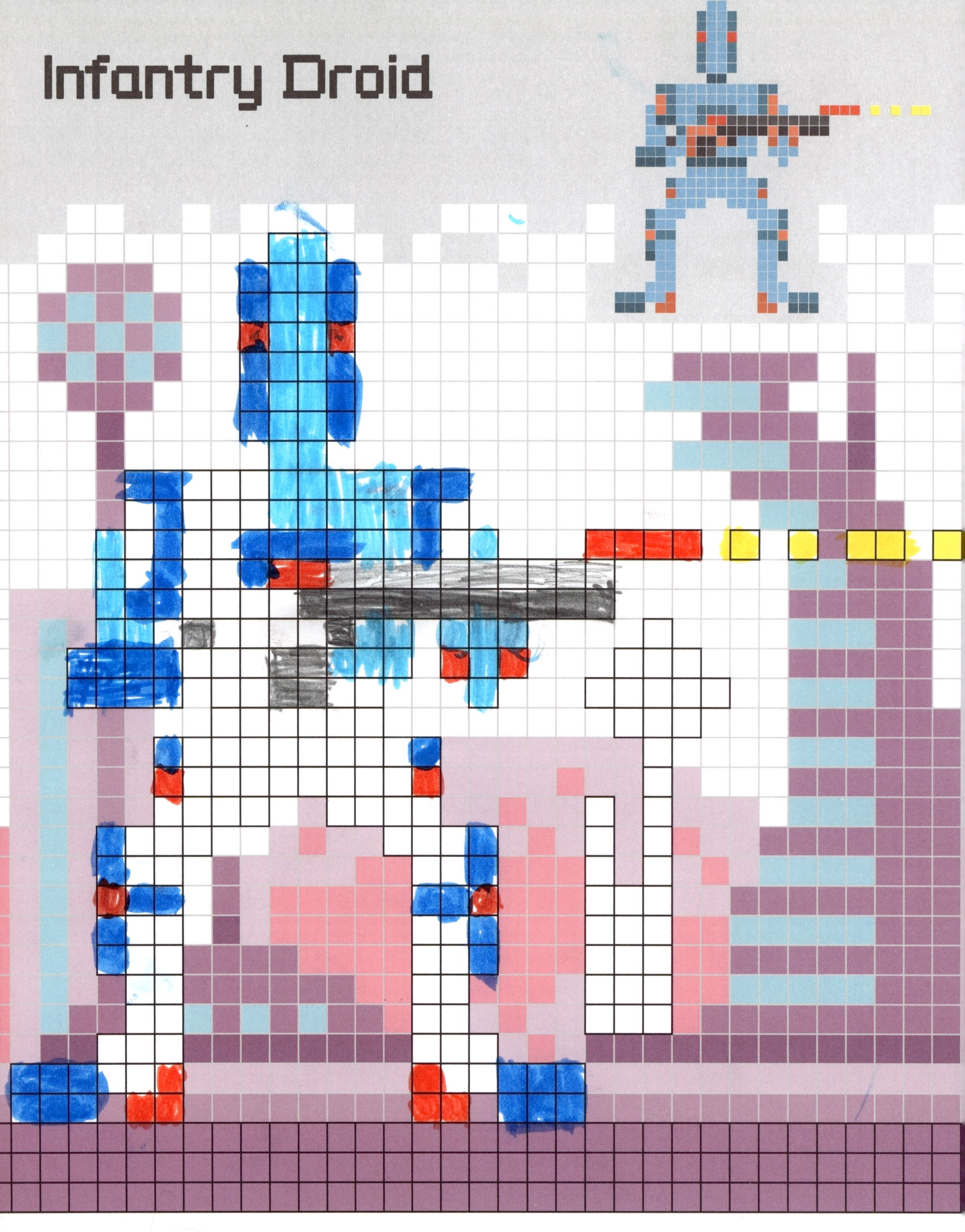

Infantry droids are the Battle Fleet's shock troops. They can fight in any environment and they never give up. Zap! Zap! Whirr ... Zap!

Vampoid

Vampoid stalks the dark edge of the solar system, looking for prey.

Shoot Out!

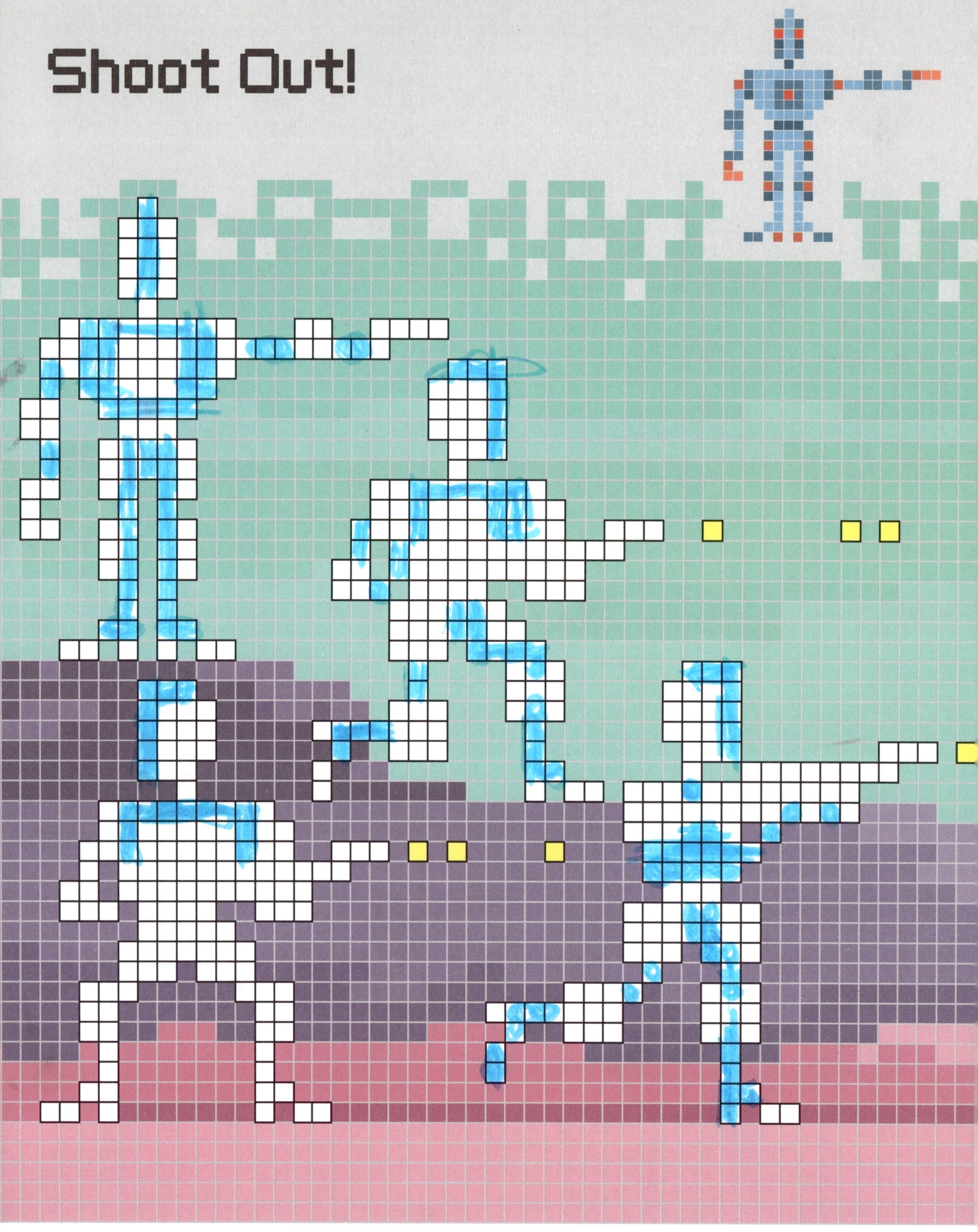

Lord Blob has been found, and infantry droids have been sent to take him captive. But his Blobbiness won't come without a fight! Ka-pow! Ka-pow!

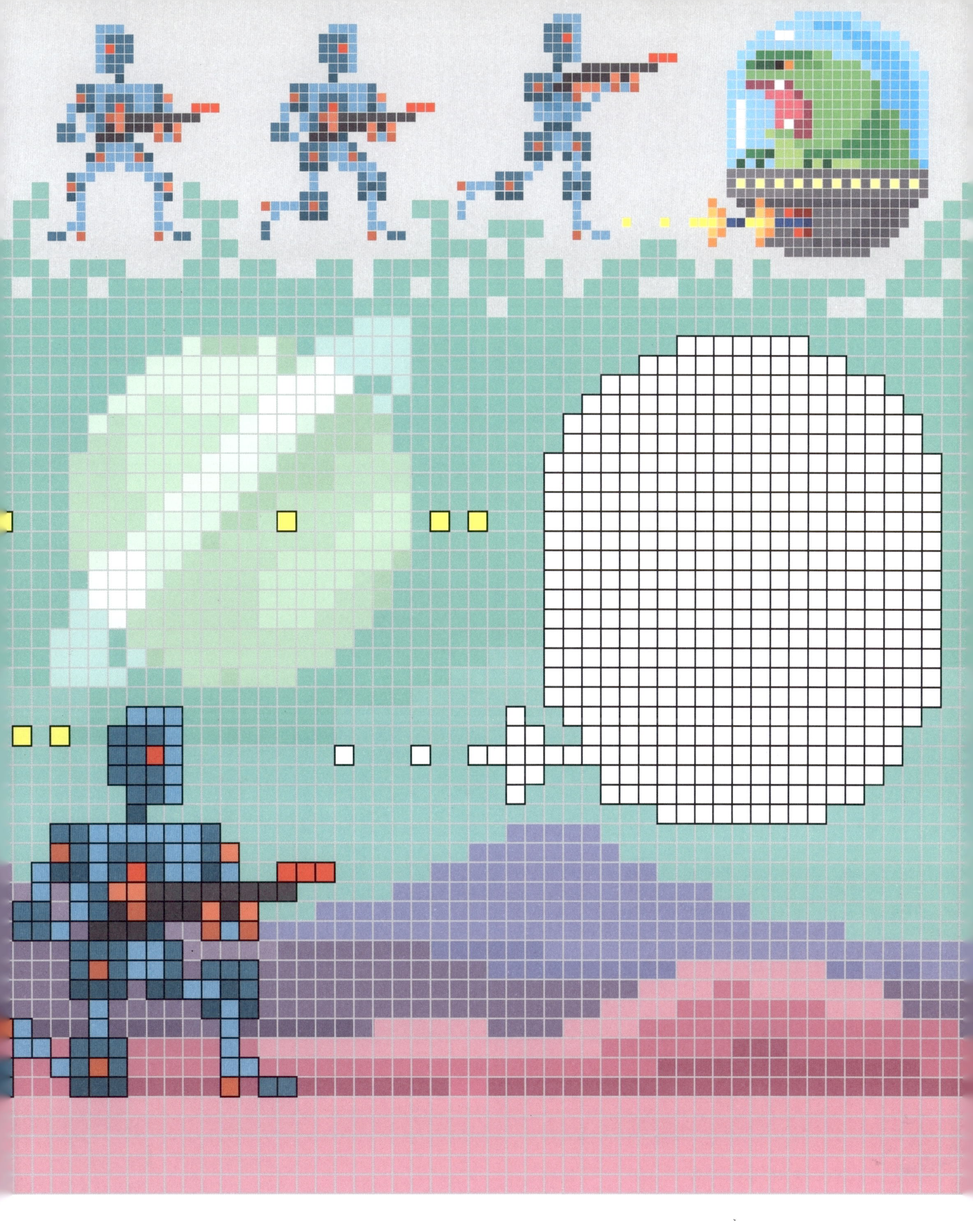

Fly Past

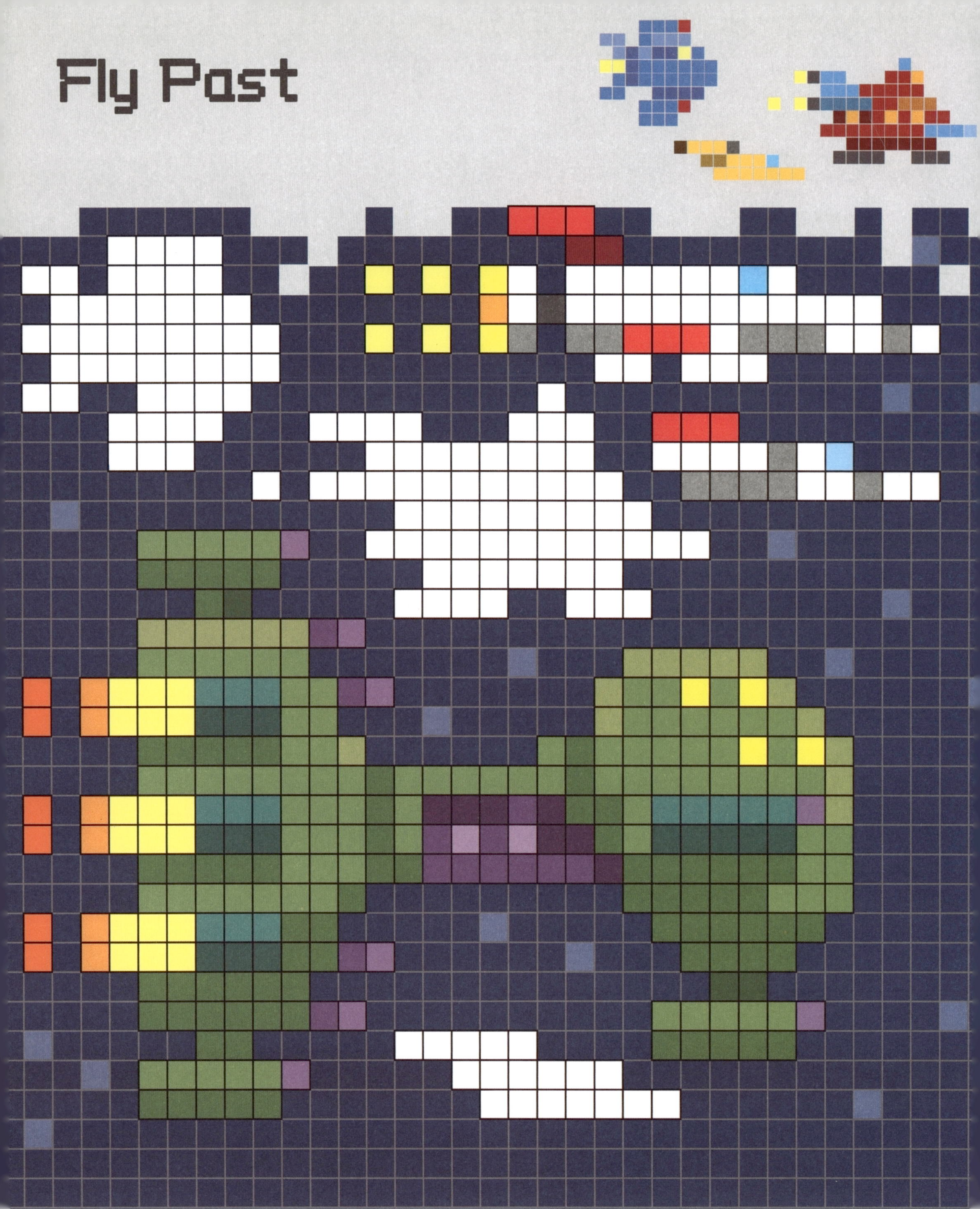

The galaxy is safe again! There's a triumphant fly past of Battle Fleet ships! Hip hip hooray!